COMMUNITY · CONNECTIONS

HOW DO THEY HELP?
THE WORLD HEALTH ORGANIZATION

BY KATIE MARSICO

CHERRY LAKE Publishing

Published in the United States of America by Cherry Lake Publishing
Ann Arbor, Michigan
www.cherrylakepublishing.com

Content Adviser: Cynthia Rathinasamy, Master of Public Policy, Concentration in
International Development, Gerald R. Ford School of Public Policy,
The University of Michigan, Ann Arbor, MI
Reading Adviser: Marla Conn, ReadAbility, Inc.

Photo Credits: ©HIRDA Himilo Relief and Development Association/http://www.flickr.com/
CC-BY-2.0, cover, 1, 13; ©L. Kraft / SuSanA (Sustainable Sanitation Alliance)/
http://www.flickr.com/CC-BY-2.0, 5 ©UN Photo/Devra Berkowitz, 7; ©Julien Harneis/
http://www.flickr.com/CC-BY-SA 2.0, 9, 17; ©UN Photo/AS, 11; ©UN Photo/
Eskinder Debebe, 15; ©Chuck Simmins/http://www.flickr.com/CC-BY-2.0, 19;
©UN Photo/Olivier Chassot, 21

LIBRARY OF CONGRESS CATALOGING-IN-PUBLICATION DATA
Marsico, Katie, 1980–
  World Health Organization (WHO) / by Katie Marsico.
     pages cm. — (Community connections)
  Includes bibliographical references and index.
  ISBN 978-1-63188-030-8 (hardcover) — ISBN 978-1-63188-073-5 (pbk.) —
ISBN 978-1-63188-116-9 (pdf) — ISBN 978-1-63188-159-6 (ebook)
  1. World Health Organization–Juvenile literature. 2. Public health–International
cooperation–Juvenile literature. 3. World health–Juvenile literature. I. Title.
  RA432.M37 2015
  362.1—dc23   2014006182

Cherry Lake Publishing would like to acknowledge the
work of The Partnership for 21st Century Skills. Please
visit www.p21.org for more information.

Printed in the United States of America
Corporate Graphics Inc.

THE WORLD HEALTH ORGANIZATION

CONTENTS

WORKING FOR WORLDWIDE HEALTH

You probably have water that comes out of a faucet and toilets that flush. However, less than half of the people living in the African country of Ethiopia have access to water.

Without indoor plumbing, it's harder to get fresh water for drinking, bathing, and using the bathroom. People in areas without

People from many parts of the world lack electricity and running water in their homes.

4

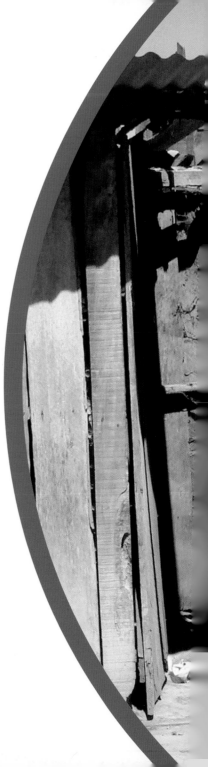

Think about how your life would be different without running water. Think about the many ways that having no indoor plumbing affects health.

easy access to clean water are more likely to have serious health issues.

The World Health Organization (WHO) develops and supports projects that improve plumbing.

WHO is part of the United Nations (UN). It carries out research that provides information about **international** health issues. WHO also creates worldwide **standards** and

WHO and UN officials meet with many organizations working to help others.

Are you able to guess what the UN is? If you said it's an international organization, you'd be right! The UN is a group of 193 world nations. These countries work together to support peace and fight hunger, disease, and poverty.

7

programs that lead to better health care, hygiene, and sanitation.

WHO has offices in 150 countries, including several **developing countries**. People in these areas often face poverty, violence, disasters, and **epidemics**. Some experience discrimination, or unfair treatment, because of their background or beliefs. Such challenges make it more difficult to stay well and receive important medical services.

Basic health care helps improve an entire community.

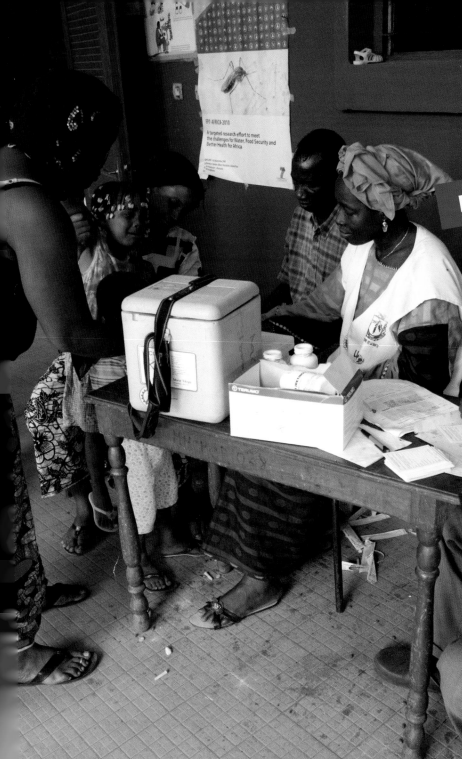

LOOK!

Go online with a parent, teacher, or other adult. Look for photos and articles that discuss different communities that work with WHO. What health challenges do these areas face? What is WHO doing to help them?

FROM 1948 ONWARD

Following World War II, world leaders formed the UN. One of their earliest goals was to oversee international health issues. This is what led UN officials to create WHO in 1948.

At first, WHO focused on controlling outbreaks of diseases such as **malaria**. It took steps to improve worldwide health care for women and children, too. WHO also

Clean drinking water helps keep people healthy.

What international health issues were people thinking about in 1948? How are they different from the health topics that WHO deals with today?

helped develop better standards of sanitation and **nutrition**.

Over time, WHO provided children across the globe with medicine and **vaccinations** against many different diseases. WHO educated the public about the dangers of drug and alcohol use, as well. It also taught people how pollution affects health.

Today, more than 7,000 men and women from more than 150 countries work for WHO.

Vaccinations stop outbreaks of disease.

Are you able to guess how WHO affords so many international health projects? If you said that money comes from a few different groups, you'd be right! National governments provide part of WHO's funding. So do other organizations that work to support people's health, safety, and well-being.

13

WHO depends on different types of workers. Doctors, **engineers**, and sanitation experts are a few examples. So are people who carry out studies on international health issues. WHO also relies on employees who prepare for and respond to emergencies.

Certain WHO workers oversee how funds are collected and used. Finally, some workers are responsible for building relationships with other groups and organizations.

WHO employees meet to celebrate their work and plan future projects.

ASK QUESTIONS!

What organizations does WHO work with? Some, such as the United Nations Children's Fund (UNICEF), are part of the UN, too. Others are government groups, such as the U.S. Environmental Protection Agency and Environment Canada.

15

HOW WHO OPERATES

One of WHO's most important jobs is to gather information. WHO then uses this research to set new health standards.

Thanks to WHO, people across the world are learning the best ways to care for unborn babies. They're finding out how to prevent health problems such as measles and poor nutrition.

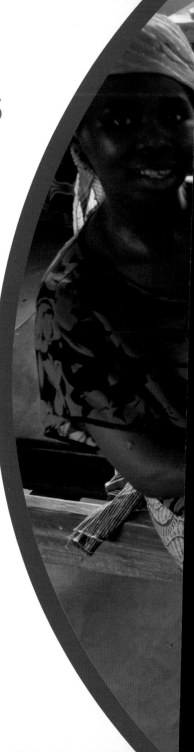

WHO provides mothers information on what to do when their children are sick.

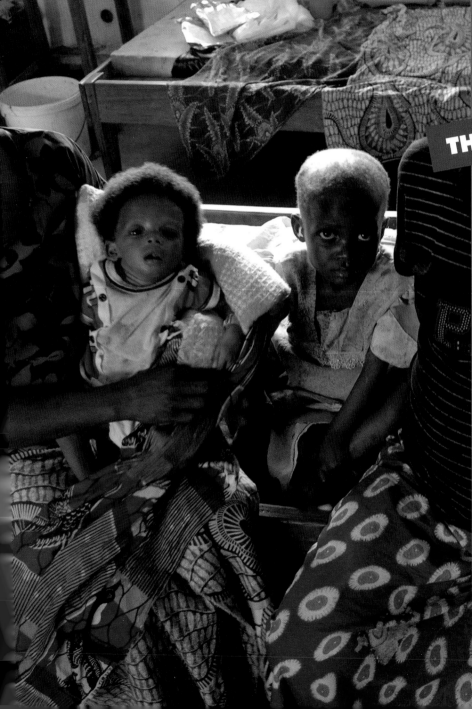

THINK!

Think about what it means to "set new health standards." One example is WHO's child growth standards. These help doctors be more aware of children who aren't growing properly.

WHO also supports programs that provide communities with vaccinations and medical supplies.

WHO develops sanitation projects, too. Workers help communities create programs to collect trash and get clean water. They teach residents the importance of hand washing and other good hygiene habits.

WHO helps make communities around the world safer places to live.

LOOK!

Head to your local library or go online with an adult. Look for photos of communities affected by air and water pollution. What health issues do you think these environmental problems create?

WHO also educates the public about how behavior affects health. Workers spread the word about the dangers of smoking, alcohol, and drug use.

They encourage people to protect the environment, as well. WHO provides information on how air and water pollution lead to a variety of health problems. WHO gives people everywhere hope of leading longer, healthier lives in cleaner, safer communities.

People all over the world benefit from WHO's many ideas for improvement.

Create your own World Health Day celebration! Every year, people use April 7 to think about international health issues and organizations such as WHO. Do the same by asking your teachers and friends to help plan special activities at your school.

21

GLOSSARY

developing countries (dih-VEH-luh-ping KUHN-treez) countries that are often poor and that are working to develop more modern businesses and social practices

engineers (en-juh-NIRZ) people with scientific training who develop machines, systems, and structures

epidemics (ep-i-DEM-iks) illnesses affecting a large number of people at the same time in the same area

international (in-tuhr-NAH-shuh-nuhl) involving two or more countries

malaria (muh-LER-ee-uh) a serious disease that causes fever and chills and that is spread by mosquitoes

nutrition (noo-TRIH-shuhn) the process of eating the right foods in order to grow and stay healthy

poverty (PAH-vuhr-tee) the state of being poor

standards (STAN-duhrdz) levels of quality that are viewed as acceptable or desirable

vaccinations (vak-suh-NAY-shuhnz) shots that protect people against various diseases

FIND OUT MORE

BOOKS

Barnhill, Kelly Regan. *Do You Know Where Your Water Has Been? The Disgusting Story Behind What You're Drinking.* Mankato, MN: Capstone Press, 2009.

Connolly, Sean. *The World Health Organization.* Mankato, MN: Black Rabbit Books, 2009.

Ellis, Carol. *Vaccines.* New York: Marshall Cavendish Benchmark, 2012.

WEB SITES

KidsHealth
kidshealth.org/kid
Check out this Web page to view articles on hygiene and other issues that affect kids' health.

United Nations—CyberSchoolBus
cyberschoolbus.un.org
Visit this Web site for more information on topics connected to world health, including poverty, hunger, and the importance of clean water.

INDEX

ABOUT THE AUTHOR

Katie Marsico is the author of more than 150 children's books. She lives in a suburb of Chicago, Illinois, with her husband and children.